'If you have ever been disadv
confidence or self-doubt then *Yal*
offers a three-step guide to maste
control of your own confidence, allowing you
of your dreams with your own authentic style of self-
belief.'

Hal Elrod,
international keynote speaker and best-selling author
of *The Miracle Morning* and *The Miracle Equation*

Dear Lorna,

Magic happens just
outside your comfort
zone!

Sarah
X

Yabadabadoit

You versus confidence – who wins?

This guide has been produced to enable you
to achieve and challenge yourself every time
you have a battle with your confidence.

Sarah Foster

ISBN: 9798585757617

PublishNation
www.publishnation.co.uk

Contents

Foreword

by Esther Stanhope – The Impact Guru
International Speaker and Award-Winning Author of
'Goodbye Glossophobia – Banish Your Fear of Public Speaking'

When Sarah approached me to write the foreword of this book *"Yabadabadoit"* about confidence and how to get it, I jumped at the chance.

Thank you, Sarah, for asking and thank you for writing this.

First of all, we have a lot in common, we both have teenage daughters and we've both struggled with confidence in our professional lives. We both love Madonna, although I'm a little older and where Sarah's first single was from the material girl herself, mine was *'Fame'* by Irene Cara in 1982!

Confidence? Oh yes, that's my bag. Sarah and I both share a passion. We love to help boost confidence wherever we go because we've experienced how valuable it is in work and life. We also both know how damaging it can be if your confidence gets knocked, smashed or squeezed out of you.

You might think I am SUPER confident…come on, I'm an international speaker, I speak live on stages and across the airwaves to thousands of people tuning in at one time. I speak about imposter syndrome and inner confidence all over the world within global organisations.

However, I wasn't always comfortable as a public speaker. And I've learnt that most people suffer from that fear too.

Even Prince Harry hates public speaking. 75% of us fear standing in front of a crowd (or on camera) with all eyes on us.

That's why I wrote my book *"Goodbye Glossophobia – banish your fear of public speaking"* . It helps people stretch their comfort zone and overcome their anxiety when it comes to speaking up and being in the spotlight.

Like Sarah, I have struggled with confidence my whole life. I've had turbo charged periods of coming across as 'overconfident' (like Sarah's Radio 1 Roadshow appearance aged 5 – you'll love that story in the book).

I too have been "paralysed by fear" and been knocked back many times in my career.

Sarah works in a corporate environment – and often finds herself sitting round boardroom tables surrounded by older and more experienced male colleagues. She's experienced working in a high-profile Football club and she's learnt that some environments can totally knock her confidence.

I too have learnt from bitter experience that, if you ignore the fundamental tools you need to grow in confidence – you are in danger of spiralling downwards and damaging your self-belief long term – which can sabotage your career prospects and …..well, your life! Yes, I know. This is important stuff!

Here's a quick story of when I experienced a professional confidence crisis when I was at the BBC…

Confession. I messed up. My confidence was totally crushed because I hadn't worked on all the things Sarah talks about in this book!

As a senior producer at the BBC in London, I was technically brilliant at my job. Picture this. I was busy. During one radio breakfast show in London you'd have at least 12-14 guests. You'd have Boris Johnson (when he was mayor of London) one minute and the next you'd have British Prime Minister at the time David Cameron. Maybe a Hollywood star like George Clooney would be needing a quick briefing (hmmm yes, nice) or Chef Gordan Ramsey needed to be supervised with a sharp knife to cut a piece of meat he'd brought in. I was in the thick of it, calling the shots, in control, and respected for my competencies!

However, when it came to stepping outside my comfort zone and stepping up to become a leader, I cracked. I was asked to go for a more senior management role, and this involved an interview. The role I was going for was the 'Assistant Editor' (they called it the ASS-ED – sounds a bit rude!). Well, I totally stuffed it up.

My boss had told me *"It's just the usual BBC interview with the usual panel, you know, it's just part of the internal HR process…you just need to go through the motions"*

So, my naïve self didn't think to get help, get coaching, spend time on myself, my value, my personal development, the panel or interview techniques. Instead, I mistakenly thought, that my 'technical brilliance' would see me sail through the *"usual BBC panel"* interview because my on-the-job experience would be enough to get me promoted pronto.

Well. On the day, the interview was at 10am. That morning, I produced the breakfast show live from 6am to 9am. That meant I got my usual car at 4am to the studio and did more or less a whole shift before the panel interview. I cringe when I think about how little I prepared for that interview.

I am embarrassed to confess now, that I was criminally under prepared and had NO idea of what was about to happen to my brain and my confidence. I didn't have the toolkit to be able to sit in front of 6 senior people, yes 6 (including two from HR, the boss, his boss, the editor and the existing ASS-ED). OMG it was awful. It was one of the worst experiences of my life.

At one point they asked me a question, and not only could I not answer with a brilliant example, my nerves got the better of me and for a few seconds I forget how to speak English (that's my one and only language).

Now I know about cortisol (the stress hormone) and I know about *"lizard brain"* and what happens when anxiety hits you – you may know about the fight, flight or freeze concept. That day, I froze.

My anxiety grew and my confidence drained out of my body until I was a quivering wreck. Did I get promoted?

No.

On that occasion I didn't, and was left with a huge dent in my confidence. It took me a long time to build it back up. But I did.

The good news? I have learnt how to build inner confidence and even better, how to help others build inner confidence. (Gosh, I wish I'd read this book then).

One takeaway from this panel failure? You CAN build your confidence back up. You have to move on, dust yourself off, learn, and go on to the next thing. WOW, I have spent so long beating myself up. Please, take it from me, beating yourself up isn't helpful.

What I love about Sarah's book is her ability to share her stories of confidence crisis' and articulate her easy-to-adopt methods to boost it back up. I can totally relate to Sarah.

This book is full of tangible and practical tips like her mantra:

Prepare – Do – Review!

Her tips and strategies are tried, tested, simple, yet life changing.

I love her chapters and advice; breathe, visualise, be grateful, focus on your PB - Personal Best (I always say compare and despair), reinvent yourself. And my favourite Sarah-ish motto ......**keep it real!**

Sarah's created a really usable personal development toolkit with a refreshingly modern and down to earth twist.

Remember, she works in a professional environment every day and knows first-hand how to put these tips into practice.

It's fantastic that Sarah has chosen to share her confidence tips and strategies with the world. This book is important as it has a message to women and girls…

You are not alone. If you feel unconfident, you are normal.

You CAN build yourself up and if you get knocked down, you can build yourself back up again if you know how.

This book will help you do that!

Confidence is like a muscle. It can be flexed and worked. So read this book, flex those confidence muscles, be brave, get out there and like Sarah says ....*yabadabadoit!*

The word WINNER
is an emotive one

Is it a good word? Does it have a down side? Here is a question: when you hear the word 'winner', how does that make you feel?

Let me pose a scenario.

Let's imagine two people – we will call them John and Rachel – who have vastly different stories.

Rachel has made herself a fortune by building a business from scratch selling fast fashion online. She has all the trappings of wealth. She has the big house, complete with en-suite master bedroom and walk-in wardrobe, and the swimming pool. She looks great every day with her designer clothes and Botox and fillers.

John has no money and lives in a small rented room in a shared occupancy house. He gets his clothes from charity shops but is always well groomed and presentable, as well as articulate and well-spoken. John used to be a car thief and a drug dealer who, after a spell in prison, turned his life around and became a youth worker. He has spent the last five years working with deprived kids in a poor area of the city he lives in, and in that time has helped two young adults who had no hope when they met him into good jobs with prospects.

John and Rachel are both WINNERS. But who is the biggest winner?

What do you think?

For someone to win, does it mean that someone has to lose? Surely neither of these two could be classed as a loser!

Let's switch the word WINNER for the word ACHIEVER! To *achieve* means that no one loses; there is no downside to achieving.

Winners? Losers? I am not sure it's in our gift to always win.

Achievers? We can always be those, *all of us.*

Lessons from our elders

Many years ago, my late stepfather had an appointment with an optician and found himself in the city centre with some time to spare. He was sitting on a bench enjoying the sunshine and got chatting to a street cleaner. My stepfather was the kind of guy who would strike up a conversation with anyone about anything!

Curious, he began to ask how the man got into that line of work. The street cleaner, whilst sweeping up litter and debris, told my dad that he had started as a binman. On his first day, he'd asked if there was any training.

'No,' he was told. 'You just pick it up as you go along.'

He told my dad that this was his regular part of the city centre now and that he hoped that when he went home at night the streets looked the best they could. What the guy meant was that he had DONE the best that he could, and that is all any of us can ask of ourselves.

When was the last time you stopped and asked yourself to do the best that you could? Is it a daily practice? A regular discipline?

When I was in my final year at high school, I had a part-time job at a care home and I often got chatting to some of the residents. In fact, my favourite part of the job was listening to the tales that the people we looked after shared with me.

As an inquisitive, nosey, naïve and, as you will soon find out, somewhat confident adolescent, one of the questions I asked was, 'Do you have any regrets?' The answer was often 'I wish I had followed my dreams more' or 'I wish I hadn't cared what others thought so much' or 'I wish I had been more confident'.

I was struck by the significance of these answers, to have reached that stage of life and to have those sort of reflections. I vowed as a teenager to be the best that I could be, and have absolutely no regrets in spite of whatever life has had in store for me.

I have often heard it said, 'You will regret the things you didn't do, far more than the things you did.' I think there is a message in that saying that rings true.

The person we owe most to in this life is not our boss, our partner, our kids, our parents or our friends, but **ourselves**. We all have 'comfort zones' that we work within (and quite like to stay in as much as we can), but to be the best we can be means getting outside those zones and achieving.

If you have ever completed a challenge, no matter the size of the obstacle you had to overcome, you will know that there is no better feeling than the moment you realise you have achieved it.

How difficult is it to end each day saying, 'Today I have been the best that I could be and I am going to be the same tomorrow and every day!' *No regrets!*

Before we move on, I leave you with this thought from Basil Fawlty that I would like you to stop and contemplate. It's from *Fawlty Towers*, I think from season two, episode one. Any fans of the show may well recognise it – it is Basil being typically Basil Fawlty! For those who haven't seen it, I am sure you could find this scene online. It goes like this:

'*Zoom.*'

'What was that?'

'Was your life, mate.'

'Oh, that was quick. Do I get another?'

'Sorry, mate, no you do not.'

It begins (and ends)
with you

Early last year I was half listening to a podcast whilst doing my ironing. This particular podcast is broadcast by a successful author, the writer of an uplifting text about applying a morning routine to improve your life. The format it takes is often that of the author chatting with, and semi-interviewing, inspirational people – people with a story to tell, people who have achieved their goals.

During the podcast, either the host or his guest (possibly both, I can't remember) talked about how you need to have lots of followers and be pictured with famous people in order to sell lots of books. You need lots of likes on social media, lots of contacts in your email marketing list, be visible in the public eye, that kind of thing.

Whilst I don't remember who said it first, what I do recall are the exact words in the podcast: 'People only buy books from people that they think are special.' I think people buy books for all kinds of reasons, and I also think the subject of a book is as much a draw as the author.

In my opinion, having read a great many books, it's the knowledge and your ability as a reader to interpret and implement teachings from the content of books that is special. We people are all special, right? As we have already explored, we all have the power within us to be winners in our own way and in our own right, just like John and Rachel. One is a successful entrepreneur, one a youth worker, but both are special, both authentic, both winners!

We all have our purpose in life. What makes us 'special' is uncovering that purpose and overcoming any confidence issues that prevent us showcasing it to its full potential.

As much as I was inspired by the author, his book and his inspiring guests, with the utmost respect I have to disagree with what was said in that particular podcast. In some ways this venture, my first book, will test out my theory!

For want of a better descriptive category, the book you are reading right now is best classified as a self-help book. I have read many such books (I hasten to add that one of the best I have read is the one written by the author I refer to above). They usually start off by validating the author. They will tell you how they came from rags to riches, have built up **multi-million-dollar**[1] companies, made it to the big time against all the odds, have multiple academic achievements, PhDs, MBAs or suchlike.

Of course, that's inspiring. I can testify that it gets you motivated to be the best you can be, to be tuned in to the flavour of the genre, to be inspired by great leaders and to find the best version of yourself.

---

[1] Sorry, but experience has taught me that America publishes self-inspiration and self-belief books like no other country so it *is* more often **dollars** than pounds, dirham, euros, yen, roubles, rupees, etc. Although let me add as a caveat that self-belief and inspirational texts can be found in many guises in every part of the globe!

However, it isn't appropriate here. I have very little desire to be followed on social media by anyone other than genuine friends, colleagues, suppliers, clients or acquaintances. I have no interest in having a large contact list or celebrity allies. What I want is to serve, to share, to help, to reach out to other 'ordinary' people who are making their way through life's rich tapestry.

Let me be clear: experience has taught me that there is nothing more important than human connections and I don't advocate shunning them. I crave knowledge, and to acquire knowledge it is essential to meet new people and listen to them and share experiences. I just don't believe that I need to have ten thousand followers or a million likes to make real connections.

That said, if you have such a following and are happy with it, good for you. If you do not, you can achieve great things just the same, so good for you, too!

By *my own* measures, I have achieved in life. I have a rewarding career, loving family, a great support network, peace and contentment in my life, and a gorgeous Labrador called Leo. Oh, and to bring me back to my point, I have harvested the confidence to be, do, say and act exactly as my heart desires. That, people, is what I am compelled to share with you! The freedom that authenticity gives you when you harvest the confidence to fuel your fullest life is, I believe, where success and achievement can be found for all. So, as I wrote at the start of this chapter, it begins (and ends) with you.

During the time you spend reading this book, make no apologies for thinking of yourself, your growth, your journey, your confidence, your self-belief and your authenticity. It's a cold harsh fact that you came in to this world alone and you will likely leave it the same way, so get comfortable with investing in yourself and creating a mindset you can rely on; don't apologise for being, doing, saying and acting exactly as your heart desires. You are the only dependable ally you have who will be with you every moment to conquer whatever life throws at you.

By the way, I highly recommend reading as many books as you can. Books about creating a morning routine can be very valuable. I think it was Mark Twain who said 'To be able to read and not to read gives you no advantage over someone who cannot read', or something to that effect. We can all agree with that sentiment. It reminds me of another quote which feels fitting here: 'if you don't use it, you lose it'.

Before we proceed, I will tell you a little bit more about who I am and, most importantly, why I am compelled to share the techniques that make up this book with anyone who might gain something positive from them. My ultimate goal in life is not to sell a million copies or receive bestseller awards (although I will take all of that graciously and with open arms if ever it comes my way!).

What I really want is for someone to say *'Because of you, I did that'*. Before we proceed together on this journey of building confidence, please remember my objective. If anything in this book inspires you to make a change that allows you to venture somewhere you haven't been before, or maybe to conquer something you have held back from, please contact me and let me know. I would be very grateful.

I firmly believe that your output and value to the world and to the environment we all share directly relates to your self-belief. If you feel empowered and confident, you can achieve whatever you set out to accomplish.

People talk about realising their full potential, but is there really such a thing? **Does it not make more sense that one's potential is infinite, constantly growing and evolving?**

Testament to this is the world we live in today. You only have to look back a few short years to see how quickly we can grow, evolve and stretch the boundaries of man's accomplishments. Perhaps the simplest example is that of an athlete setting new records and constantly breaking old ones. I have several friends who enjoy taking part in triathlons and they regularly tell me about beating and exceeding their personal bests, often referred to as PBs. Growth and capabilities are infinite if you allow yourself to practise the art of authenticity by harvesting your inner confidence to achieve whatever you want to achieve. Trust me when I tell you, it is in there!

The origins of your
inner confidence

I was born confident. One of my very earliest memories was getting up on stage at a roadshow (for those too young to remember the roadshows of the 1980s, think of a music festival held in daylight hours that was typically organised by a radio station). It was a Radio One roadshow and, to the best of my mum's recollection, it was summer 1985 or 1986 which would make me four or five years old at the time.

There were thousands of people watching live bands on a large stage hosted by the radio station DJs. It was a great atmosphere, with the crowd singing along, dancing and enjoying a carefree vibe. During a break in the music, there was a competition with the host asking for volunteers to come on stage to see who could do the best pop star performance.

At the tender age of four or five, I just knew I had to get up there, where the bright lights were, above all the people in the crowd. So, as my mum looked on in shock, I bolted off, elbowed my way up to the front, waving and shouting to be picked. I was helped over the barrier and onto the stage. I was asked my name and where I was from and handed a blow-up guitar, before proceeding to give the performance of a lifetime.

To this day, I can remember feeling so very proud of myself for getting on the same stage as the bands and receiving applause from the crowd, who obviously thought I was very sweet (the blow-up guitar was probably bigger than I was). They cheered for me to win the competition, which I did.

I felt elation and pride, standing up there in the spotlight. In contrast, my mum confesses she was panicking as she battled her way through the crowds to the front of the stage so she could retrieve me safely and take me back to our tartan picnic blanket!

It was the same event, the same moment in time, but we had such different reactions and feelings. My internal voice at four or five years old said, 'Yes, you can! Life is for living. Go get on the stage where the bright lights are and shine (with your blow-up air guitar and in exchange for the prize of a Radio One car sticker!).'

We will come back to why this roadshow is my anchor in harvesting inner confidence. First, I want to be clear that during the years I was coming of age, whilst I could give you many examples of me stepping up and expressing myself and feeling great while I did so, there were many times when I was literally paralysed by fear. It stopped me right in my tracks and sometimes came out of nowhere. I have been too shy to speak out even when I knew that my contribution would be valid, and failed to put myself forward despite being sure I could do a task well.

Have you ever felt like that?

Ten years ago, I started a new job at a premier league football club. It was my responsibility to sell corporate hospitality, and a large part of the job was to network with high-net worth individuals as well as senior decision makers from profitable large companies.

By that stage in life, I had a solid track record of networking. I had built a successful sales career, first in the telecommunications industry just as mobile technology was emerging, and then in advertising during the economically favourable years at the turn of the millennium. I was an experienced senior sales person with a track record of annihilating my sales targets through effective networking and building relationships. Everyone who had met me (including my new employers) had absolutely no doubt that, if there was the opportunity to network and have business conversations that would lead to a deal, I was the girl to get the job done.

As such, I was given the task of attending a corporate event at the club with the sole purpose of speaking to as many people as I could and exchanging business cards to build a pipeline of leads. On paper, this was a relatively easy task for me; these people were at a famous club, they were interested to hear about our facilities and hospitality, and receptive to talking with someone who could offer them an exclusive tour of the stadium and the potential to claim a stake in the ground on match days and share the club's success. It was an exciting task and I had the world at my feet in my brand-new job, so off I went from my office to the conference area ready for the task at hand.

Sadly, I did not return with many business cards or leads; in fact, I spent most of the event hiding in the toilets. Fear set in as soon as I entered the room full of people. For whatever reason, I was overwhelmed and unable to open my mouth and engage in conversation with anyone.

There was no easily identifiable trigger for my reaction. It wasn't that they were an unfriendly or intimidating bunch, but something within stopped me in my tracks. My urge to hide was so strong that I could not fight it. It was a far cry from the Radio One stage I had inhabited so gloriously some years earlier! I felt fear, I felt miserable, I felt I had failed. Imposter syndrome had established its stronghold.

After that incident (which was not the first nor the last of its kind), I started to make a real effort to notice when my confidence levels were low and when they were high. As a young and ambitious employee, I started to study my confidence so that I could formulate my own coping strategies. I was never going to subject myself to imprisonment in a toilet cubicle again!

As an observer or 'student' of my own, seemingly paradoxical, application of this thing we call confidence, I have come to understand it. I recognise the warning signs when confidence is low, call it out and rectify my belief systems just in time, at that crucial point before the atelophobia sets in and my self-limiting version of myself robs me of my accomplishments.

Faith: establish
your anchor

The dictionary defines confidence as: 'the feeling or belief that one can have faith in or rely on someone or something'.

I have learned that the way we, as humans, build trust or faith is through our experiences. At a basic level, we use our senses for this. For example, if we eat some food that we particularly dislike, we will be very cautious when we see food that resembles it again. When we're offered food similar to that which we know we don't like, we may not even try it because our frame of reference tells us we don't like 'that type' of food.

On the other hand, if we find a food we enjoy we will usually be quick to try anything that resembles it. We will expect more of the same – something that we like. More than once, I have picked up what I thought was a chocolate-chip cookie, only to take an excited bite and realise it is full of dried fruit, not my beloved chocolate chips. If you have ever had a similar experience, you will know that having a mouth full of something you didn't expect, particularly if it is something you dislike, is uncomfortable!

In psychology this type of behaviour is comparable with 'classical conditioning' which, for all intents and purposes, could be simply interpreted as 'learning by association'. The influence of learning by association can be strong, deep-rooted and invoke responses such as nausea, anger and phobias – also known as fear!

For those of us fortunate enough to have had someone patiently teach us to ride a bike when we were young, we probably started with stabilisers to help us with balance. To only have two wheels would have been uncomfortable (a bit like a mouthful of unexpected raisins or a conference room full of strangers!). It was likely to cause panic and fear, or a response like, 'It's okay – I don't need to learn to ride a bike. I will just walk or maybe get a scooter instead.'

As time went on, we will have been encouraged to try without the stabilisers. Our instinct, if we were **brave** enough to take that next step, would be to ask our mentor, be it mum, dad, an older sibling, friend or family member, to hold on to the back of the bike seat and walk at the rear while we pedalled. Perhaps we didn't quite **trust in our ability** not to fall off the bike. Perhaps we had seen others fall off, or given it a try already and fallen off ourselves. Perhaps we felt unstable, so our instinct was telling us we wouldn't be okay if we didn't have someone holding on to the back of the bike and steadying it.

So maybe now we are confidently pedalling, safe in the knowledge that someone is holding on and we will not fall. For me at this point, my dad did what many parents do and let go without saying a word. A nanosecond later came my realisation that I was doing it, I was riding the bike all by my super-proud little self! I could do it all along and thus faith was established and I pedalled like I have never pedalled before, the wind against my face and a sense of freedom I had never felt before. Interestingly, thirtysomething years on, there is not much that is *less* scary to me than getting on a bike and riding it. I do it on autopilot, without giving it a second thought.

Riding a bike for the first time, like most things in life that require you to be **brave** and **trust in your ability**, takes a bit of patience as well as harnessing your confidence. Whilst it isn't essential, it helps if you have someone reliable and patient at your side.

This is where your anchor that I mentioned previously comes in. Remember my little rock-star self, up on stage at four or five years old? Whenever my confidence comes into question, I remind myself that the little rock star with her blow-up guitar lives within me; we are one and the same. Her bravery and the trust she had in her own ability are inside the person I am today. They are *my* bravery and *my* trust in my own ability.

To end this chapter, let's do some work to establish your anchor of faith in your own confidence.

Take a moment to write down a few of your accomplishments in life that required you to be brave and trust in your ability. What have been your proudest moments so far? Take as long as you need and write down as many or as few as you want. They may be things like riding a bike, completing a challenge for charity, making a special dinner for a number of family members or friends, going for a promotion, learning to swim, stepping up and taking a penalty for your team, being interviewed for a new role, taking an exam, learning to drive, becoming a parent, getting on stage to sing, putting your hand up in a class, networking in a room full of people, asking someone out on a date, volunteering to take on a new project, introducing yourself to someone new maybe on your first day at school or college or at a new place of work...

I will stop here, but hopefully you have enough inspiration to take a few moments to congratulate yourself on your accomplishments, large, small and everything in between, that found you expressing your confidence, achieving and being authentically you!

_____

_____

_____

_____

_____

_____

_____

_____

_____

_____

_____

_____

_____

_____

_____

_____

_____

Once you have written down a few things, fold the corner of this page. If you ever doubt your confidence or have a wobble about how much you can achieve, come back to it and remind yourself how capable you are!

Here lies your anchor. You can use it as an achievement log too, so every time you do something new that has challenged you to be brave and trust in your ability, write it down, celebrate it and take pride in the knowledge that you are an achiever. As time goes by, I have no doubt that you will need to continue on extra paper in a new notepad.

Keeping it simple,
keeping it real

We live in a complex and sometimes confusing world. The intricacy and demands of life in the age of the fourth revolution, with smartphones, smart TVs, smart homes, smart vehicles and even smart cities, are sometimes tricky to navigate, and there seems to be a growing consensus that 'switching off' in our technology-led era is more difficult than ever before.

Recharging is essential to your wellbeing, and your wellbeing is essential to being brave and trusting in your ability; consequently, recharging should be a regular practice if you are to stay on the path of achieving your goals and realising your dreams.

Recent experience has taught me that if you need to take a break, recharge or 'switch-off' in order to check in with your own wellbeing, it's the simple things that will reap the biggest dividends. Fresh air, the great outdoors, writing in your diary, walking the dog, doing some exercise you enjoy, reading a book or even taking an impromptu nap! Look around you and you won't have to look far to be convinced that some of the best things in life are simple, well-kept little secrets for us to uncover like hidden treasure.

As luck would have it, the art of authenticity through harvesting your inner confidence is simple; in fact, I have come to believe that most cognitive actions or challenges relating to shifting one's mindset can be broken down in to **three simple practices**.

In my day job as a company director, I recently developed a coaching session for some colleagues around 'handling difficult conversations on the telephone'. The purpose of this was to adequately prepare my colleagues who were faced with the challenge of delivering news to clients that the cost of complying with a particular piece of government legislation was increasing sharply. Because of the nature and mechanism of the route to compliance, the clients would either have to pay the high, unbudgeted fees or risk non-compliance and potential enforcement action. Not an easy telephone call to make, but a necessary one nonetheless.

The tools that you need to equip you for handling difficult telephone conversations are no different to the tools required for anything else that fills you with trepidation, be it proposing to your loved one, going for a promotion, taking a career change or delivering a public speech.

Although picking up a phone, dialling a number and having a conversation are three things that, in their own right, are very straightforward and 'easy' to do, for many colleagues over the years conducting a telephone conversation has proved one of the most feared actions in the workplace. I have seen people procrastinate and put them off time and time again. Have *you* ever put off making a call?

Interestingly, we now have alternative forms of communication to make things easier – you can send an email or message instead. But there are still some instances where picking up the phone will get you the best result.

I believe the three practices we are about to break down and master together can be applied to overcome all of the regular conundrums that life throws at you.

As we have already discovered, this procrastination is caused by the fear of something going wrong or, more succinctly, fear of failure otherwise known as 'atychiphobia'. According to my good friend and research assistant Mr Google: *'Atychiphobia is the abnormal, unwarranted, and persistent fear of failure. As with many phobias, atychiphobia often leads to a constricted lifestyle, and is particularly devastating for its effects on a person's willingness to attempt certain activities.'*

As much as I am indebted to my research assistant, I am going to call out the above definition as harsh!

There are two words that make it so: 'abnormal' and 'unwarranted'. As my paradoxical experience of being both confident enough to rock out on a stage in front of thousands of people and tremble on a closed toilet seat in a locked cubicle shows, when it comes to fear of failure there is no 'normal'. I know from experience that when the fear sets in, it certainly does not *feel* 'unwarranted'; in fact, I would say it's about as real a feeling as you can get. It is often accompanied by very real physical symptoms such as involuntary fidgeting, sweating, trembling, not to mention your heart beating at ten thousand beats an hour!

So, for the purpose of this book which is designed to help you find your most confident self, I will put forward a revised definition for our own personal use:

According to me: '*Atychiphobia is a word we can use to describe the common fear of failure that arises in most human beings at some or many points in their lives. As with many phobias, atychiphobia can be overcome. It does, however, take a commitment to bravery, trust in oneself and mastering the application of three straightforward practices.*'

No-one, absolutely no-one, should leave this earth having lived a restricted life, a life with 'devastating effects', as cited in my trusted researcher's definition. Can we work together to ensure that this doesn't happen? If you are on board and would like to be a part of the confidence revolution, then please read on!

Three practices
to remember

Confidence is something that has fascinated me for as long as I can remember, perhaps because I was referred to as confident so many times during my childhood. As I have already remarked, I was 'born with it'.

Or was I?

I had no hesitation in communicating with others, speaking my mind and asking for what I wanted from an early age. I would hear my mum's friends, say 'Isn't she confident?' and she would reply, 'Oh yes, nothing fazes her.' I would be compared to my sister in that regard, and it was expected that if one of us needed to put ourselves forward it would most likely be me, the 'confident one'.

Adults would remark, 'She is not shy, is she?' I heard this from teachers, neighbours, family and friends from a very early age, so you might say I was labelled confident before I even understood the concept. Consequently, there is a part of me that truly believes I showed up as confident as a child, because that was what I'd been labelled as. It was what clever adults expected me to be and they had clearly made up their minds that I was.

Looking back now, after many years of trying to understand why confidence is such a powerful tool and after many life experiences, I believe that my quieter, more reserved big sister was probably born with as much confidence as I was. To challenge a viewpoint I held, and look at confidence from a different perspective, I am not sure that anyone is 'born with it' or 'not born with it'.

Was I acting confidently as a child because I was born that way, or because everyone expected it from me and so I conformed to their expectations?

Is how much confidence you have the luck of the draw? What do you think? Do you have any experiences that suggest how your experiences in those early years have shaped how confident (or not) you feel today?

Maybe it's easier for some people to believe that confidence is something you are born with because that means you can relinquish any accountability for a lack of confidence. If you believe you were born without confidence and that's just the way it is, there is nothing you can do about it, right? It's simply the hand you were dealt. That's a nice, easy and neat way to justify staying in your comfort zone. But, given you are reading this book to help you increase your levels of confidence, I'm guessing that you aren't in that camp and you don't want 'easy'!

Like many other characteristics and attributes, I believe confidence levels can expand and contract depending on how we are feeling and what our belief systems are at any given moment.

I often hear the term 'having a crisis of confidence'. I have used the term myself, and I am testament to the fact that confidence can be high and low in the same person. If confidence is something that people can have a 'crisis' of, then they must also be able to have a 'confidence breakthrough'. This is a term I hear much less frequently. Maybe we should remedy that; let's make 'breakthroughs in confidence' commonplace.

Breakthroughs in confidence should be celebrated; if you have one, no matter how small, make sure you acknowledge it and congratulate yourself. This is something that will make your confidence 'muscle' expand, making it easier for you to harness confidence when you need it to carry out a particular task or achieve a goal.

It's worth remembering that word 'achiever' again, because confidence and achievement tend to go hand in hand. The more confident you are, the more you will achieve; the more you achieve, the more confident you will be. Confidence and achievement feed off each other and grow together over time.

What if we can attain confidence breakthroughs whenever we choose to by using three simple practices? Would that be something worth exploring?

The words 'practice/practise' here are key. You generally get better at things when you practise them regularly; if you practise enough, you master the art. You may have heard the 'ten-thousand hours rule', which is the idea that to become world class at something requires ten-thousand hours of dedicated practice. Assuming you practise something for eight hours per day, seven days per week, 365 days per year, it would take you roughly three-and-a-half years to become world class. For some, that may be an overwhelming prospect. It would be quite a commitment, would it not, to practise something every day for over three years? It would require so much dedication and an unwavering focus on the end result.

I choose to look at self-improvement in a different way. In my view, practising the art of confidence is best approached with the compound effect in mind. The compound effect is the strategy of getting from where you are to where you want to be through small, simple, regular actions performed consistently.

I firmly believe that it doesn't matter how many hours you spend; all that matters is that you practise consistently. If you can adopt the practices into your routine then all the better, as you will then be practising them daily. Over time, they will become part of your belief system, which will make them habits so they will be always there for you, serving to harness your authentic inner-confidence whenever and wherever you happen to need it.

1)   **Prepare**
2)   *Yabadaba* **Do** *it*
3)   **Review**

These practices are simple in that they are easy to understand and recall: Prepare, Do, Review (PDR for short). They are simple to understand and learn, but that is not to be confused with easy to execute.

What I should declare at this stage is that the work needed to make them change things for you and uncover that glorious and authentic inner confidence probably won't be easy. Like everything worth having in life, there will be varying degrees of graft, blood, sweat and tears (metaphorically speaking, of course). How easily the three practices pan out for you will depend on the obstacle you are trying to overcome, the timing, and your wellbeing at the time.

These practices are also a habit you will need to form; you will need to adopt them. By working on your confidence, you will also work positively on your mindset. If this sounds like it's for you, and you are prepared to take the path that may not always be easy, I promise that these new habits will serve you unconditionally for a lifetime!

Prepare

My stepfather often used to say to me, 'Fail to prepare, prepare to fail, Sarah, for preparation is the key.' As a teenager I would look at him quizzically and nod with a smile, ever fond of him and grateful for his wisdom. I consider myself extremely lucky because he was a great mentor as I grew up, sharing many anecdotes and wise words that have served me well. But that phrase in particular was often used with sincerity and in an array of different contexts in our household.

I believe those words to be one of his greatest gifts to me. They have helped me to perform at my best in countless situations over the years. In essence, they sum up why practice number one is in fact practice number one *of three*, and why it has to come right at the beginning.

Another frequently repeated saying in our household was: 'Change the way you look at things and the things you are looking at will change.' It took me until adulthood to understand that sufficiently to put it into practice. Where harnessing your confidence is concerned, both of these mantras are worth remembering.

If your memory is a sieve like mine often is, jot them down in your diary or make a note of them on your phone. If there is a rebel in you, find a pen and underline or highlight them on this page before folding over the corner. (Maybe not if it's a library book or borrowed copy – though why not?!)

Planning and preparation have proved to be useful tools in many aspects of life. Since the dawn of time, the human race has applied them to achieve all manner of greatness. Effective planning and preparation are at the root of many everyday essential tasks. The teacher will plan and prepare for the successful lesson in school; the construction company doesn't forge ahead with a new building without plans and the right tools at hand. A well-delivered speech has often been written, edited, recited and practised before it's delivered to the listeners.

Our ancestors used planning and preparation to conquer nations and to win on battlefields. More recently, planned research and development is eradicating disease and increasing life expectancy though the advancement of medical science.

So how do we prepare effectively to be more confident? Is it really possible to 'plan and prepare' against atychiphobia setting in, like it did for me when I was instructed by my boss to go and talk to some potential clients? Let's explore that question.

The power of visualisation

The first step to planning and preparing anything is to visualise. You may have heard the adage 'start with the end in mind'; that's exactly how to prepare when it comes to harnessing the confidence within you. How do you want the situation to pan out? How do you want to feel? What reaction do you want from others? What's your ideal? Start with the end in mind, for this will give you your 'why'.

Take the example of giving a presentation or a speech. This is something that I have seen people get anxious about time and again; it's something that has made my own heart race more than once. Be it a presentation to colleagues, your teacher, your boss, a client, a supplier or even the guests when you are delivering the speech at a wedding or retirement party, speaking publicly is something that will often get people questioning their confidence or ability to deliver. In the instant you agree to it (or worse, are elected for it/told you are doing it!) your natural reaction is to question your abilities.

All eyes and ears will be upon you. Some of the questions that may arise internally are:

What if you miss the train and you are late?

What if you forget what to say?

What if you trip over and fall flat on your face?

What if you get a tickly throat?

What if you say the wrong word?

What if the wrong word is a rude word and you offend people?

Worse still, what if you inadvertently swear?

What if you spit as you talk?

What if you go red in the face?

What if you get too hot?

What if you get too cold?

What if there's a power cut and you're plunged into darkness?

What if technology fails you and your presentation slides won't run or, worse still, the wrong presentation opens on your screen, or your holiday snaps from Ibiza?

How embarrassing!! What if all these things happen one after the other and everyone starts laughing or staring blankly? All staring blankly at *you*. How will you ever recover the situation? What will you do? How will you cope?

You may be smiling as you read this, but these are all thoughts I recall having. Reading them now as I write, whilst I'm obviously not under any pressure to prepare for a presentation or a speech, the words 'unlikely', 'far-fetched', 'absurd', 'improbable', 'inconceivable', 'doubtful' and 'you are being a bit of a drama queen, aren't you, Sarah?' spring to mind.

However, these are all thoughts that I have had at one time or another! Worse still, they are all thoughts that I have visualised, and when you visualise something it can invoke powerful emotions, powerful enough for you to run and hide (or maybe lock yourself in a toilet cubicle!).

If visualisation is such a powerful tool and it arises from our thoughts, let's go one step back, take control of those thoughts and change the vision. They are *our* thoughts, after all, so we get a say in them. If you can change your mind, you can change your thoughts, right?

This is where that helpful saying that you have remembered, written down or underlined in this book comes in to play: **'Change the way you look at things and the things you are looking at will change'.** We can translate it here to: 'Change your thoughts about the presentation you're going to give and the way you feel about the presentation will change'. In other words, call yourself out and flip it!

If your original thought about something that you want or need to do is unhelpful and takes you down the path of fear, notice it. Be on the look-out for it and have a little internal chat with yourself about it. Put the record straight.

We are going to explore the notion of chatting with yourself in more detail. How often do you give yourself a pep-talk? If it's not often, you may wish to schedule a pep-talk with yourself soon. Talking to yourself is one of the best and quickest ways to empower a confidence breakthrough.

Q) What's the difference between the person feeling a little anxious about giving the presentation and the person who is confident and ready to deliver the presentation of their life?

A) It's not that the latter is a better person, more capable, stronger, smarter, etc. It's largely down to the way each person has visualised the presentation panning out.

So, if you have a presentation to deliver, take a deep breath and visualise the outcome. Whatever your personal fears about delivering it, make a conscious effort to think the opposite. Have positive mantras ready to rehearse in your mind to quieten any unhelpful chatter.

Instead of letting your mind scare you with thoughts of 'what if I forget what to say?' let's visualise this: 'I remember everything I want to say because I know the subject matter and I will invest time in learning my presentation'. Literally talk out loud, loudly and adamantly, over the inner negative chatter. Then imagine the presentation going well and you delivering it, remembering what to say, improvising, pausing for breath and smiling!

Instead of 'what if my audience aren't engaged?' let's visualise this: 'My audience will listen to what I have to say because I will make sure I am engaging and the content is relevant.'

In my experience, visualisation and combatting negative mental chatter takes a bit of practice (be mindful of the power of practice in all that you do – instant results are a rarity, maybe even a myth!). The power of visualisation is something you need to be consciously aware of; if you get into the habit of visualising that things will turn out as you want them to, over time they will.

When my teenage daughter went back to school last year after the summer break, I could tell that she was anxious the night before her first day back. New school year, new teacher, new timetable, the start of working towards her exams. My instinct was to try and reassure her with practical things, such as letting her know where her lunch money was, ensuring her uniform was clean, ironed and hanging neatly where she would expect to find it in her wardrobe, and asking her what time she would like waking up in the morning.

She asked if she could Facetime her friend before bed. As she did, I overheard them sharing how nervous they felt and how they wished that they had more time off and the school holidays weren't coming to an end.

How lovely that they have each other for support when they are feeling a lack of confidence. I am going to come on to the power of besties (and why you are your own bestie) shortly, but my reason for sharing this particular event is a little more specific. Over breakfast the next morning, I asked her how she was feeling. 'I am okay,' she said. 'I was talking to Abbie about it last night on Facetime and she told me that she'd stood in front of the mirror and said to herself "I can do this, it will be okay", so that's what I have been telling myself and now I'm feeling okay.'

It's a simple mantra but it worked, and when shared with a friend it became twice as powerful. All Abbie had done was notice her thoughts about feeling nervous and not ready to go back to school. She'd observed them, realised they weren't serving her and changed them, consciously changing her inner dialogue and **visualising** that the day would be okay, that *she* would be okay. And guess what? They were both okay on their first day back.

The power of habit forming

I have shared a little about my career. My time in sales early on in my working life taught me a lot about human nature. I spent a number of years working in the advertising industry when media was evolving at a pace. The way we can seek and absorb knowledge and information has already changed beyond recognition in my lifetime.

When print media was in decline and the internet was surpassing traditional means of advertising, we often discussed with advertisers how people are habit forming. For instance, there was a generation who had always looked in a phone book if they needed a tradesman, so it was important for tradesmen to have a presence both in a phone book and on the internet to capture maximum response.

Humans are habit forming. Creating new habits is how we evolve and, I believe, how each generation becomes stronger, wealthier and 'greater' than the previous one. I will state that again: *I believe human beings become stronger, wealthier and greater through forming new habits.*

To form new habits, such as the habit of visualising positive outcomes and overcoming negative mental chatter, there are a few key ingredients that will make it easier: **purpose, drive, willpower** and **discipline**. These ingredients can be added to your psychological mixing bowl to create the perfect recipe for achievement.

Purpose is personal and has to come from your soul. Drive will come naturally from within if your purpose is strong enough. Willpower and discipline are the things on which you must consciously rate your performance and bring back in check if you stray from your path. If this is all starting to sound a bit 'woo-woo', fear not; when we break it down below it will make sense.

Purpose

This is simply your reason. Why bother? Why bother going for promotion? Why bother delivering the presentation? Why bother joining the fitness club? Why bother climbing a mountain? Why bother starting your own business?

One of the most important questions we can ask ourselves is: 'What matters to me and why does it matter?'

Purpose is personal. What will be the rewards of doing the thing that is scaring you? Will you be wealthier, stronger, smarter, happier, more content?

The American entrepreneur, author and motivational speaker, Jim Rohn famously said that the reason he became a millionaire was (in retrospect) 'for the person he became' once he'd made his millions. Jim also shared that he lost the first fortune he amassed but, because of the person he had become in getting there, it wasn't difficult for him to do it again. After losing his millions, he got them back and was even wealthier the second time around. He had a strong, clear purpose, something that mattered to him.

My purpose in writing this rather than having a lie-in at weekends is to prove to myself that I can do it, and to satisfy my desire to have at least one person say to me, 'Because of you, I did that! I overcame a confidence crisis, got on with it, have been working with the three practices and it's working out great!'

Perhaps the real question to ponder, rather than 'Why bother?' is 'Why not?'. If we use a common example of putting yourself forward for promotion, why *shouldn't* you try and achieve it? How will you feel further down the track if you don't? If you don't go for that promotion, at some stage it's likely that someone else will, so don't you owe it to yourself to step up? We are all capable of more than we think we are.

I think Eminem sums it up best in 'Lose Yourself' with the opening lyrics which essentially ask the question 'If you had one shot to get everything you want, what would you do?' Do you seize it, or do you let it slip away? I recommend going and listening to these opening lyrics anytime you need a shot of motivation or you are questioning whether or not to go for something you want in life.

If you want the promotion, you have to try. If your instinct is that you can do the job, then really think about the purpose. At the risk of repeating myself to hammer home the point here, in your one short and precious existence you really do owe it to yourself to try, to go for what you want in life. Remember what we established at the very start of this book: 'Achievers – we can all be those, all of us!'

Think about the worst that can happen, acknowledge it, then choose to think about and really focus on the **best that can happen** and get in that camp. Visualise the best that can happen. I assure you, you have nothing to lose!

Once you can envisage the best that can happen, that is your 'why'! You fully deserve, and are capable of, that best-case scenario and all of the rewards that come with it. Hold on to your purpose and allow yourself to get excited about the great things that will come now that you have your 'why'.

Drive

If you have arrived at your purpose and it is strong (i.e. something that your heart desires), it will feed your soul. It is something that matters to you, so drive should come more easily. Just keep reminding yourself of the purpose, the reason, the benefits that will come; keep visualising the best that could happen and you should remain driven to achieve it.

A useful aid is keeping a journal. Write down what you want and why you want it in a notebook. Do this repeatedly and regularly so your purpose is never far from your thoughts.

During a difficult time in my personal and working life in my mid-twenties, my line manager (who was a great mentor) told me that your feelings become your thoughts, your thoughts become your words, your words become your actions and your actions create your reality. Positivity is the key to staying driven.

Positive feelings and optimism are a choice. I'm not saying that they are easy to switch on; it can take a tremendous amount of energy to 'look on the bright side' or 'find the silver lining' or be 'a glass half full'. But I believe we have the potential to get there if our purpose is strong enough, no matter how many curve balls are thrown at us.

There will be times when life throws something at us hard, so hard that we are knocked sideways, and positivity is knocked out of us and is nowhere to be found. During these moments it's okay to go through the necessary emotions of processing the issue, and to take whatever time is necessary to heal and get back to our positive state.

Maybe you are going through one of those times right now, or have done recently. If that's the case, I'm sending you blessings and good wishes from the bottom of my heart. Even if it's hard, you will get through it because nothing in life is truly constant; everything is always moving and re-shaping. Difficult times always pave the way for kinder times. Like the seasons or the weather, difficult times do and will pass.

To carry on my stepfather's legacy of having an inspirational quote for every occasion, let me share my all-time, number-one favourite. I recite this often to my children (and anyone else who happens to be in earshot). It is one that I came across a few years ago when I read a book by Viktor Frankl called *Man's Search for Meaning*.

I read the book on an aeroplane on the way to Krakow, on a trip I took with my husband to visit Auschwitz and pay our respects by understanding what happened there. I highly recommend the book, and I highly recommend the trip if you have the opportunity to go.

I am not ashamed to admit that I sobbed openly on the plane; the book it is not an easy read. You may well have heard the quote: *'the last of human freedoms is to choose one's attitude in any given set of circumstances.'* It is profound and it is relevant in harnessing your confidence: choose to be brave, choose to believe in yourself, even if the circumstances are scary. Choose the right attitude for success.

Like Viktor, and many other philosophers and those with a keen interest in mindset work, I believe we can harness the power to overcome adversity that we encounter in our own time and our own way. When we do, purpose and drive often propel us forward to greatness that could only come through experiencing our troubles.

I have witnessed many times that challenges present opportunities and obstacles are necessary detours in the right direction, but we often forget such truths when we are under pressure. We need to hardwire them in to our thinking so that we are conscious of them even when we are under pressure.

So there we go, back to habits. How can you make thinking such positive thoughts a habit?

The same manager who told me that your feelings become your thoughts, your thoughts become your words, your words become your actions and your actions create your reality, also gave me a hack for harnessing my drive. I still use it to this day. She recommended that I wrote things to myself on Post-it notes and stuck them on my sun-visor in my car so that I would see them each time I was on my way to a sales meeting. I wrote things that were positive: my goals for the day; how I wanted to show up in order to overcome challenges, and how much sales revenue I intended to achieve. I still do this but, given that I work from home a lot more now, I stick the notes on my bathroom mirror so I am reminded morning and evening whilst brushing my teeth what my values are, who I want to show up as and what I am working towards.

The phrase 'like a phoenix rising out of the ashes' signifies emerging from a catastrophe stronger, smarter and more powerful. It's a phrase I have used many times to describe someone very close to me who has battled against more than her fair share of adversity in life. I marvel every time she comes back fighting. I dedicate this paragraph to her and also to you, if it resonates with you.

Remember, there is always a purpose to come back fighting – when you are ready, of course.

If you can make a really conscious effort to stay positive, then positive feelings will become positive thoughts that become positive language that inspires positive actions. *Et voilà* – you have a positive reality.

Be the powerful phoenix that you are.

Willpower

Willpower is something that you have to be completely conscious of. Anyone who has ever been on a diet will know that you have to be very conscious of your ability to resist temptation. You can't afford to take awareness away from what you are and are not eating for any length of time.

I was told recently that about 80% of brain action is carried out by the subconscious. If that is true, most of the time we are going through life on autopilot! To exercise willpower effectively, we need to engage with ourselves internally to constantly challenge our initial thoughts, feelings and reactions to carry out our own sense check. If we habitually question our natural responses, we learn to verify whether we are serving our own best interests. The real test of willpower comes after the initial gloss of the purpose has worn of.

If you have been side-tracked at this point, or even forgotten why we are delving in to these key ingredients of purpose, drive, willpower and discipline, you can be forgiven because I have gone off at a slight tangent. As a reminder, we are exploring what it takes to form good habits simply because we need to get into the habit of preparing effectively. If we get into a habit, it will be much easier to stay on track and stay on the path of harnessing our most confident self.

We have explored the concept of how, rather than reaching our full potential, we are always growing and evolving towards our infinite potential. Being aware of, and sticking with, that concept, even when the going gets tough and it would be more desirable to take the easy path back in to your nice little comfort zone, is all wrapped up in how you apply your willpower.

I will state that again: *how you consciously use your willpower will determine how much and how quickly you grow and evolve towards infinite potential.*

If the going gets tough and you have a wobble, ask yourself: 'Am I wielding my willpower right now to be the best that I can be?'

You could think of these key ingredients as your helpers, little warriors that are on your team, that have your back. They all have different skills that complement each other to lead you to victory.

- Purpose leads from the front on your quest to achieve.
- Drive keeps everyone informed of the purpose whilst making sure everyone is on track and stays motivated.
- Willpower keeps the team of warriors focussed on the end goal and diverts them from distractions.
- Discipline gets everyone up every day, trains the team and makes sure that they follow the codes of behaviour required to serve your desired results.

You have the troops within you to win on any personal battlefield so, if you have a crisis of confidence, remind yourself of this and call in the cavalry!

Discipline

Discipline is the ingredient that carries out the training and dedication to the cause, in this case to form the habit. It is like the glue that holds everything together.

In the context of helping us form habits, discipline can be summed up as 'regular practice'. Many people who use an alarm to wake up during the week so that they are at work on time will not set the alarm on their days off. For instance, they may set their alarm for 6.30am from Monday to Friday but not set it on Saturday and Sunday. They may find, over time, that they begin to wake naturally at 6.30am on their days off despite no alarm sounding. Of course, they may then choose to pull the covers over their heads and try to fall asleep again, but their natural reaction (even if they went to bed at a later time than they would in the week) is clear evidence of regular practice, or discipline, forming a habit.

Practice is a word that features heavily in this book. We have all heard the saying 'practice makes perfect'.

Does practice make perfect?

I'm not sure it does

Do we even need it to?

I suspect not.

What practice will do is help us become better and take us from apprentice to master over time.

Be your own bestie

When harnessing your inner confidence so that you can achieve all that your heart desires, it's beneficial to have people rooting for you.

Imagine your best friend or a close family member is having a crisis of confidence. Let's imagine that they have failed their driving test twice and have booked it for the third time. They really need to pass this time because they want to progress at work to a role that includes some travel, and they cannot apply without a full driving licence. Or maybe their eldest child is due to start school soon and it isn't in walking distance or on a public transport route, so they need to pass their driving test to do the school run.

They haven't told anyone but you that the third test is booked because they don't want to have to explain yet another failure if things don't go well on the day. What would you say to them in this scenario?

I would place a bet that it would be something along the lines of the following:

- 'You can do it, you are ready'
- 'Third time lucky. Good luck, you will do great'
- 'I am rooting for you; this is your time now'

rather than:

- 'You have already failed twice. What if you fail again?'
- 'What if the instructor doesn't like you?'
- 'What if all the bad drivers are on the road that day and someone causes you to have an accident?'

I am confident about this because we wouldn't keep our friendships or relationships intact if we made the last three statements to our nearest and dearest. Indeed, we are unlikely to let others speak to us like that, just as we are unlikely to speak to those close to us in that way. Why would we want to upset them? How would such negativity help them?

And yet so many of us take a negative approach when chatting to ourselves internally. As we have already explored, we often berate ourselves with our self-talk. If you look at the statements above then apply the situation to yourself rather than a friend or family member, is it the first three that spring to mind that will be your internal mental chatter when the test is approaching?

Hands up anyone who immediately thought of one of the latter three statements if it was your own test and you had already failed it twice.

If your hand is raised now, you are not alone. When we explore the second step, 'Yabadaba**Do**it', we will examine why we are likely to have negative internal chatter when we encounter a challenge or something new, and where all that negativity comes from.

Try and be aware of any negative self-talk. When you notice it, form a positive response to yourself.

Whenever my kids say anything negative about themselves, whether they are speaking directly to me or whether I overhear it, I immediately ask them to counter it with three positive things about themselves. I do this because I want them to be their own besties. As they prepare for what the world holds, I want to be sure that they have their own backs and are strong and confident enough to overcome whatever life has in store for them.

To give an example of how this goes down, it can be something as simple as 'I am no good at maths'.

I will insist upon them finding three positive statements, which might go along the lines of:

- 'I am trying my best at maths, despite it not coming easily to me.'
- 'I always complete my maths homework and hand it in on time.'
- 'I am a lot better at maths now than I was when I started school.'

It's great when you have a good support network and people on the sidelines cheering you on as you succeed. It is also extremely fulfilling to cheer on the people around you, encouraging them to achieve and do well. But where harnessing your own confidence is concerned, it is personal; it's got to come from within you as well as from others around you.

It is human nature to problem solve, so many of us are great at giving advice. We sit and listen to the dilemmas of those close to us and gently guide them towards making a choice that helps solve their problem. By being our own bestie, we must get into the habit of doing this for ourselves, too.

If you have travelled on an aeroplane, you'll know that during the safety briefing you are told to put on your own mask before helping anyone who needs assistance with theirs. Being your own bestie is similar; if you can forge your own positive attitude, you will be better placed to serve those around you.

If you're not feeling as confident as you would like to about something, have a pep talk with yourself just as you would with someone you really care about. Imagine what you would say to them and say it to yourself multiple times with conviction. If you do this, I promise you will see positive changes in terms of your confidence.

It is no coincidence that this preparation section is a long one. It is arguably the most important of the three practices: get the preparation right and the rest will fall in to place.

Before we dive into to the second step, lets recap step one: Prepare.

It is my hope that you are now equipped to plan for increased levels of confidence. The beauty of this wonderful gift of life is that we are all so different. We all learn differently, are inspired to take action by different things, and measure our accomplishments differently.

I am keen for you to thoroughly review what you have read so far and take note of your own top takeaways in the space provided below.

If you are struggling with where to start, I will share my own review with you and a little more about what has worked well in my experience. For me, visualisation has worked almost 100% of the time. That, coupled with getting control of my internal dialogue, have proved to be my go-to fixes. Whenever I need to harness my inner confidence, I go back to basics and I plan. This is something I would really recommend you focus on if it is brand-new to you, or if it feels uncomfortable. If you stick with it, it really is a powerful tool.

Rather than just read ahead, I implore you to spend a few moments thinking about the tools and techniques that you feel will best serve you. It's important to have these thoughts and learning to come back to, as and when you need them.

How many of us studied a second language at high school such as German, French or Spanish? We spent hours in class mastering common words, phrases and conversation starters with our pocket-sized dictionaries. I studied French in school and, although I found it one of the tougher subjects, I got a grade B so not a bad result. In fact, I could hold a decent level of conversation in French back in the day. However, with a lack of practice over the years, I now struggle beyond *Je m'appelle Sarah, j'habite en Angleterre.* Thank goodness for Google Translate, hey?

That is why it's important to summarise your key learning here so that you can come back to it when you need a refresher (like that pocket-sized dictionary).

We have considered being your own bestie, having your own inner army of purpose, drive, discipline and willpower, techniques such as visualisation, forming positive habits (and ditching any unhelpful ones), as well finding your anchor. Which of these are you inspired to use to help you grow your confidence, and how do you intend to implement them?

This may be another page you fold over or insert a bookmark to come back to. Essentially, it provides space for you to capture your own review of the importance of planning and preparation.

YabadabaDoit
in the here and now

In 1960, a new American sitcom aired called *The Flintstones*. It was an incredibly successful television show, reportedly one of the most financially successful and longest-running network animated franchises (it ran for three decades). American publication *TV Guide* rated *The Flintstones* the second greatest TV cartoon of all time, second only to *The Simpsons*.

The charm of *The Flintstones* lay in its humorous juxtaposition of modern concerns with a Stone Age setting, with Stone Age characters – dinosaurs and all! More than one hundred characters appeared in its many episodes, my favourite being a lovable character who had his fair share of 'mishaps', Fred Flintstone. Fred was often taught the lessons of life the hard way, with his desire for an easy life and taking short cuts causing him unnecessary hardship time and again.

For the most part, there was one of life's little lessons to be learnt in each episode as Fred and his family and friends overcame various challenges in the fictional town of Bedrock. All usually ended well. Perhaps the most valuable lesson came from Fred's catch-phrase: 'Yabadaba-doo!'

Fred would often use the catchphrase as a positive declaration, and it became synonymous with an expression of happiness and excitement. Ultimately, it was adopted as part of the theme song for the show. I believe that we can continue to use this as a positive expression that will remind us of the value of stepping out of our comfort zones to achieve the great things we are capable of.

Let's coin our own version of the catchphrase Yabadaba-doo!, to harness our inner confidence, to signify the link between Fred Flintstone and the reason that many of us find it difficult to rise up and to put ourselves forward. Let's 'Yabadabadoit'!

To understand the link, we'll examine confidence from a psychological viewpoint.

For many years, psychologists and psychiatrists have concluded that the human brain is wired to protect us from danger. It is widely accepted that the brain's job is to keep us safe, not happy.

You have probably come across the 'fight or flight' response. Fight or flight is a term commonly used to describe the human response to the presence of something that is either mentally or physically frightening. When presented with danger, the brain and the nervous system release hormones to prepare the body to either stay and confront the perceived threat or to run away and get to safety.

There is an abundance of research and some very interesting books that examine this matter in great depth. If you struggle with anxiety, I recommend spending time exploring fight or flight.

To give context to Yabadaba**Doing** it, we can keep it simple. In a nutshell, the term fight or flight represents the choices that our ancestors (like Fred and Wilma Flintstone) had when faced with imminent threat and danger.

They could either fight

or

They could flee.

There was also a third option: they could freeze and be completely debilitated, stuck with no control over their fate – which is possibly the most unhelpful reaction of all! No one should ever be stuck with no control over their fate; there is always a better option!

The fight or flight response was first described by American physiologist, Walter Bradford Cannon around 1915[2], when it was suggested that a chain of rapidly occurring reactions inside the body help to engage our resources to deal with threatening circumstances.

Fight or flight – in both cases, the brain's response to stress prepares your body to react to danger.

---

[2] Harvard Medical School: https://meded.hms.harvard.edu/walter-bradford-cannon

In 1915, he coined the term fight or flight to describe an animal's response to threats… He asserted that not only physical emergencies, such as blood loss from trauma, but also psychological emergencies, such as antagonistic encounters between members of the same species, evoke release of adrenaline into the bloodstream. https://en.wikipedia.org/wiki/Walter_Bradford_Cannon

The mind is so very powerful, isn't it?

We have discovered that visualisation can be powerful; it therefore stands to reason that the natural response to real danger will occur in the same way as in response to 'perceived' danger.

A really important question you need to ask yourself if fear sets in – and you need to be really honest when you answer it – is: **'Is the danger real?'**

I heard a statistic recently that over 90% of the things we worry about as humans never happen. I can't substantiate the statistic, but I'm inclined to believe it when I analyse my own experiences. How about you?

I would encourage you to explore whether this makes sense in terms of the things that you worry about. A great hack to build self- awareness, which in turn can help you build your authentic inner-confidence, is to keep a record of what triggers you to feel fear. Use a notepad or just add it to your notes on your phone. Whenever you experience a lack of confidence and any of the symptoms relating to fear of failure, write down what made you feel that way, then write down honestly whether it was a genuine danger.

Was it really insurmountable?

Was it a real threat?

If you are still having a wobble and you still feel under threat, even having written it down and trying to rationalise it, ask yourself: **Have I seen others overcome this fear or accomplish anything similar before?**

You are not asking yourself 'have I done it before?' (although we will come back to this in a moment), you are asking 'has it been done before?' If the answer is yes then you know it can be done – it can be Yabadaba**done**!

If it's something you have done before and you still feel nervous, ask yourself why. Did you have a bad experience previously? Remember that you are the master of your destiny and the captain of your ship.

If this happens, if nerves overcome you, go back to being your own bestie. If someone you cared about was feeling nervous, what would you say to support them? Think about it from a place of kindness, then say it to yourself.

In step one, we saw that preparation arguably takes the most time to adopt and implement in the three-step process of prepare, do and review. Preparation is the 'habit-forming' step, and forming a habit takes time, purpose, drive, willpower and discipline. Preparation requires us to be intricate, detailed and thoughtful.

Where we are now in step two, *Do*, requires you to bring a different energy – shorter, snappier, less intricate, fiery. It may sound a little unconventional, but what I want you to think about here is who you need to be at each step. Following the steps in *Yabadabadoit* will help you become more confident, but you can supercharge the effects by focusing on 'how' you follow them. Get into the right place and use the right energy; put simply, think about **the person you need to be** when you execute each of the steps.

If you have a severe lack of confidence, step two may be the one that requires the most effort and the most radical change on your part. This is the step where you don't think, you don't contemplate, you just get on and do it! With intent and commitment, you Yabadaba**Do**it.

If this is something that you find difficult, remember the compound effect we talked about. Take small steps, challenge yourself in ways that are manageable (but still outside of that comfort zone!) and build from there.

In the Stone Age when Fred Flintstone was around, it was very useful for the brain to have a built-in method of protecting us from danger or perceived danger. Life was a bit more straightforward back then. To help you picture the scene back then, stone was widely used in Fred's lifetime to make precision instruments with an edge or a point. In those days, man needed such implements in order to survive.

During Fred's time, man would rest, hunt, eat and rest again. Rest, hunt, eat, repeat. That was the secret to survival back then – a far cry from smart phones, smart homes and smart cities. There were no supermarkets to rock up to, or drive through fast-food outlets, or takeaways when you were hungry; you hunted or you starved! In between resting and eating, the main task was hunting. This was the prehistoric equivalent to your modern-day job; through hunting you received sustenance to maintain yourself.

Another essential part of survival while you were out and about maintaining yourself and avoiding starvation was to protect yourself from being hunted. Unfortunately for prehistoric man, a wide variety of species adopted humans as their prey. In the Stone Age, survival was about tuning in to any perceived danger and avoiding it to ensure you lived another day. As evolution would have it, it is from those times that we have developed the senses we have today.

So, it's easy for us to understand why it was very useful in those prehistoric times for the brain to be wired to produce an instant response to perceived or actual danger. In prehistoric times, cavemen and cavewomen were equipped to deal with threats by their bodies being primed instantly for 'fight or flight'. In prehistoric times, it was useful for your brain to be wired to keep you safe.

Your brain alerting you to possible danger is just as useful in the modern world. However, today's world is less straightforward and offers more opportunities. If we want to be safe but also be fulfilled and happy, we need to take control of the automatic response and make more judgement calls.

In simple terms, wouldn't it be better to acknowledge the primitive fight or flight response when it triggers within you and make a controlled judgement as to whether there is real, imminent danger?

It's a case of being really rational.

Is a bear going to attack you?

Are you about to fall off the edge of a cliff?

Or is the situation something that represents a challenge that you can deal with? To circle back to the key point of step two, if it's the latter then thank your brain for its natural response and tell it calmly: 'I've got this, I just need to YabadabaDoit!'

In a nutshell, challenges and dangers have changed over the years and we can change our responses to them to better suit our desired outcomes.

(I should add here that if you really are on an actual cliff edge, or a grizzly bear is angrily sizing you up, get to safety as fast as you possibly can!)

If you are squirming a little at the thought of thanking your brain and telling it you are okay because you don't want to start talking to yourself, remember that inner dialogue is happening all day long. You may as well get involved in the chat!

On the theme of internal mental chatter, in recent years, mindfulness has come in to the mainstream as a technique to improve wellbeing. If you've ever tried it, you will know just how difficult it is to quieten your mind and think of nothing. If you haven't tried it, take a moment now to see how long you can sit without thinking a single thought to yourself.

How did you get on?

Rest assured, you are already talking to yourself *a lot*. If it's happening anyway, it makes sense to actively engage in the conversation – after all, you are the boss!

For many of you, step two – 'Yabadaba*Do*ing it' – might be the hardest step. It needs the most commitment; You have to make a commitment to yourself to resolve what has caused your crisis in confidence.

'Just do it' is a powerful statement, one that is spoken often and has even been adopted as the slogan of a successful sportswear and accessories brand (you know the one!). It's much easier said than done, isn't it? But much like the athletes in the training gear beating their personal bests, if you can master it you will reap the rewards. On the other side of 'Just do it' is pride, success, fulfilment and achievement, not because you won the race but because you had a go. You proved to yourself that you have what it takes.

'Yabadabadoingit' is a little more methodical than 'Just do it'. It puts you more in control. It involves taking a few seconds to understand that your brain is wired to assess the danger in the world, just like Fred Flintstone's was. Then you must acknowledge that in the modern-day world the dangers are not as explicit as they were; despite feeling fear, you are probably safe to proceed.

As I have repeated throughout this section, it is not easy; this is the hardest step for most of us, so be prepared to work at it and have a few internal debates with your inner Fred or your inner Wilma, the prehistoric you. You will get results if you acquaint yourself with your prehistoric you; get to know and respect them and then you can negotiate. Get comfortable with having an internal chat because it's useful in overcoming anything that stops you harnessing your confidence and it can be extremely empowering. Moreover, its essential to the second step in the three-step practice.

To give you an example, here is how the internal dialogue could go if you were sitting in a waiting room before a job interview.

You: 'Uh-oh, it's nearly time to be called in for the job interview.'

Prehistoric you: 'Don't go in. Can you even remember what you want to say? How will you convince the interviewer that you are right for the job? What if they have seen better candidates already? There is clearly danger here, let's go home.'

You: 'Thanks for pointing out that it is a challenge. I appreciate you keeping me safe but I think we've got this. We have prepared, and we wouldn't have been invited for the interview if we didn't have the skills. Let's go in and see how it pans out.'

Prehistoric you: 'I am really not comfortable going in. It will be embarrassing if we are asked a question we haven't prepared for. And what if there is a really long silence? We could tell the receptionist that we are feeling unwell and then we can go home where it's safe.'

You: 'I have got your back, I promise. If there is a long pause, we can fill it by saying something. We can ask for them to repeat the question, or ask them to elaborate on what they mean while we buy time to think. We can do this, I promise it will be okay. There isn't imminent danger here, just a chance to be challenged which might lead to us getting the job.

Prehistoric you: 'It seems like you are determined to go in, so I will continue to look for any danger on your behalf and, if **I think** there is any, I will let you know again'

You: 'Thank you. Let's see how well we can do!'

As you gain experience in having chats with the prehistoric you, you'll get to know what works for you. Remember, they are in there with good intentions and genuinely trying to protect you from danger, so you need to win them over to instil calm and remind them of the modern-day reality. I find it helpful to take a parental approach, caring, reassuring and nurturing, like you would with a child.

To give it an identity, why not name your prehistoric you? Call it Fred, Wilma or anything else that feels appropriate.

As well as having honest conversations with your prehistoric you, there are a couple of other hacks that can help you in situations like the one outlined above. Let's explore them together. There is no rocket science – once again we are keeping it simple.

Breathe

We live in a 'smart' world, in which technology assists with everything from communications to logistics. I, like many others, wear a smart watch that regularly prompts me to breathe. Surely I am already breathing? Of course I am or I wouldn't be writing this, but that's not what the watch is telling me.

You see, we breathe on autopilot without thinking. My watch is encouraging me to take one minute to breathe mindfully, not on autopilot but with observation, to breathe with intention. To breathe deeply reportedly has benefits such as improved blood flow, improved posture and detoxification.

I firmly believe that deep breathing can also reset your nervous system, slowing you down when you go into 'panic' mode.

We know that when we are not confident the symptoms can include fidgeting, rapid thoughts and increased heart-rate. Can you guess what one thing you can do any time, anywhere, in any circumstance, that can help with these involuntary symptoms?

Inhale. Exhale. Repeat as needed.

Whilst studying towards his A-levels, my son was invited to an assessment day at IBM's UK head office for an apprenticeship with the company. It was a full day of pitching, presenting, skills tests, role play and questions in both group and individual settings. At the tender age of eighteen, he drove the 230 miles in his first car and a shiny new suit, full of aspiration.

With a good few weeks' notice ahead of the assessment day, we had prepared in full. We had visualised, practised his presentation, created and rehearsed his 'elevator pitch', gone through the likely questions he would be asked and rehearsed well-thought-out, interesting and relevant answers. We even thought of a memorable task he could execute so that the assessors didn't forget who he was when the day was done. He was as ready as he could be, so off he went.

I was doing what mums do and sending positive thoughts to him when, around five minutes after his assessment day had started, my phone rang. It was my son calling. I panicked a bit. Had he broken down? Run out of fuel? Got lost? Turned up on the wrong day? The answer to all these questions that ran through my mind when the phone was ringing was 'no'!

When I answered the phone, he was in a panic too, so I had to calm down. I used the same calm and collected tone I adopt when I have an internal conversation with prehistoric me!

It was clear that nerves had got to him: he felt sick, couldn't think clearly and was frozen in his car, not wanting to go in. He had already walked into reception. Looking at the other candidates, the magnitude of the building, the fact that it was his first experience of its kind – I am not sure what, but something (or a prehistoric someone, I suspect!) had led to him make an excuse about leaving something in his car and walk straight back out again.

Hours of preparation, 230 miles, a new suit, five minutes past the start time and there he was, self-imprisoned in his car. I told him we were going to breathe together. I took three deep, audible breaths and asked him to do the same whilst clearing his mind and thinking only about his breathing.

I can't recall the exact dialogue that followed, but I do remember us discussing him having two choices: start the car and drive home wondering what could have been, or have a chat with his prehistoric self and go into the building to complete the assessment day he had prepared for, as he had visualised. He did the latter, he Yabadaba**did**it.

The day was a success and he returned home late that evening brimming with achievement. He doesn't work at

IBM but he did make the cut to their matching pool on the day; this meant he was added to the list of talented candidates to be contacted for future vacancies. He was subsequently offered several apprenticeship positions to pick from by a number of organisations, after successfully attending many such assessment days. He is currently very happy working for a large firm in the city centre, enjoying a good salary and benefits whilst gaining further qualifications on the job. On occasion, I wonder how different things could be right now had he not taken those three deep breaths.

Hold your head up high

Whilst on holiday a couple of years ago, I was looking at the activities notice board in the hotel and a particular activity caught my eye: 'morning stretches'. I booked for the next day and it was my first exposure to the practice of yoga.

Our small group were given mats and we did various poses and stretches under a canopy in a beautiful, peaceful setting in the glorious Maltese sunshine. I enjoyed it so much that I went back every day of the holiday and got to know the instructor. She was incredibly passionate about posture and delivered a great hour of morning stretches each day to help us feel at our best whilst on our holidays.

She told me that she was working there for the season and had accommodation provided by the hotel. When I asked her how she spent her time off, she surprised me by telling me she read and re-read the books she had on stretching therapy and the science of flexibility to ensure that she continually improved her teachings. I'd been expecting her to say she relaxed at the beach or headed to the water park.

She impressed on me the importance of posture and I returned home after that holiday feeling half an inch taller and being very aware of not slouching but standing tall and taking up space with my presence. I have since enjoyed my own regular yoga practice (shout out to yoga with Adrienne who is fantastic and can be found on YouTube if you ever want to give it a try).

Standing or sitting tall can give you an edge. Imagine that there is a string being pulled vertically from the centre of the top of your head, keep your shoulders back and rise up. Even if only subliminally, standing tall will increase your sense of presence and help you maintain confidence. The *Cambridge Online Dictionary* captures this sentiment perfectly in its description of the well-known saying 'hold your head (up) high' by using the sentence: 'If you know you did your best, you can hold your head high' as an illustration of the meaning.

Most of us are going through life doing exactly that, trying our best with whatever life throws at us. Whatever challenges and opportunities unfold on our journey entitle us all to hold our heads up high!

Turn that frown upside down

Early on in my career, when I first started to give presentations in front of large and small audiences, I was given a valuable piece of advice. I was told, 'Smile – it's a powerful weapon.'

Now, this will take a little bit of practice as a forced, fake or false smile could be creepy and do you more harm than good! It is true, however, that smiling makes you feel good; it puts you and others around you at ease, attracts people to you and makes them feel good too. Some scientists claim that smiling can lift your mood, boost your immune system, lower stress and even make you live longer!

How does smiling make you feel? Maybe we should try it. Try lifting the corners of your mouth right now as you read this and make sure the smile reaches your eyes – a smile isn't a weapon until it reaches your eyes because that's what makes it authentic. Do you feel any different now you are smiling?

Whether you do or you don't smile right now, there is no harm in keeping up the practice of smiling. It is claimed that a smile can spur a chemical reaction in the brain, releasing hormones such as serotonin and dopamine which are said to reduce stress levels and increase happiness. If our stress levels are low and happiness levels high, we are likely to be the most confident version of ourselves.

So, do yourself a favour by smiling as much as you can. As the song goes, 'When you're smiling, when your smiling, the whole world smiles with you', so smiling is super powerful. You can pass on all the benefits described above to friends and strangers alike all day long by flashing them a genuine smile.

Hydrate

Water is essential for human life. Given that you are alive and kicking and reading this, I am guessing that you sustain yourself with liquid refreshments at regular intervals. However, many of us don't get enough hydration, which comes with a whole entourage of less than desirable side effects.

I firmly believe from my own experience that drinking water increases how alert and responsive we are. You probably know that your body is around 60% water, so it makes sense to put clean water regularly into your tank.

Drinking enough water has many reported benefits in the context of maintaining your levels of confidence. Perhaps the most significant benefit is that it forms saliva. Given that many interactions that cause a lack of confidence involve communication, it is key to ensure that your mouth and throat are lubricated so you can communicate well.

Scientists report that drinking enough water also regulates body temperature, delivers oxygen throughout the body (via the blood) and boosts skin health, not to mention that your digestive system depends upon it. It is perhaps the easiest of these hacks to implement and form as a habit; just drink water at regular intervals, simple as that!

Use music to its best advantage

There are few things in life that can alter your mood more quickly than music. The right song can motivate you, make you smile, calm you, evoke positive vibes and prepare you to take on a challenge. This is evidenced by the number of workout/running playlists and albums.

When people need to dig deep and find motivation, they often use music. When people want to set the tone or vibe in a particular moment, they use music. Music can empower us. If you have ever listened to the lyrics of a song and felt good, or maybe just the rhythm or the beat has made you feel good, then make sure you always have access to those tunes in your life for whenever you need them.

It is wise to have a motivational playlist with the music that helps you get into a positive mindset, and it is wiser still to make time to listen to it.

Our preferences in terms of the songs that empower us will differ, so explore what makes a difference to your mood. I have hundreds of songs on my motivational playlist, but a few of my personal favourites are: Christina Aguilera's 'Fighter'; Love Inc's 'You're a Superstar'; Des'ree's 'You Gotta Be'; Urban Cookie Collective's 'The Key The Secret'; M People's 'Moving on Up', 'Proud' and 'Search for the Hero'; Gwen Stefani's 'What Are You Waiting For'; Destiny's Child's 'Survivor'; The Killers 'The Man', and Survivors 'The Eye of the Tiger'.

Anchor

When I am having a confidence crisis, I take myself back to that stage in the early 1980s and remind myself that the little girl who rocked out and became an instant superstar for the day lives within me. I am her and she is me. The same skills and attributes she had that enabled her to shine are MY skills and attributes.

If you need reminding what you are capable of, flick back to the earlier chapter, *Faith, establish your anchor*, and review all the achievements you wrote down. If you skipped that exercise and didn't write anything, read it again and do it now!

Even if you are feeling short of confidence at this moment, I promise you have it in you. When you have reviewed or written your achievements, think about the person within that enabled you to achieve those things and step out of your comfort zone. That is you! Pick the example that most epitomises the level of confidence that you need for the situation you are in now and hey presto – there is your anchor.

You are an achiever and your capabilities are vast.

That confident little girl who ran to the front to get on the stage only focussed on one thing: feeling like a superstar. There is a lot to be said for focussing on one thing, especially when nerves set in. It can ground you and it can give you some perspective. For example, if you are waiting for an interview or big meeting, focus on your introduction. If you are on stage giving a presentation and feel nerves setting in, focus on a particular person and smile. If you are playing darts – focus on the triple twenty!

The art of reinvention

You may well have picked up on this already but, to give clarity to the point, harnessing your inner confidence is as much about *unlearning* as it is about *learning*. Whatever habits are holding you back from achieving the things you want to achieve have been learned, formed and cemented over time. Depending on your stage of life, they could be deep-rooted habits that have formed over several decades, in which case unlearning them and forming new and positive habits to replace them could take you some time.

Views on how long it takes to form or break a habit vary greatly: some say it takes six weeks, others longer. It's worth keeping in mind your 'why' when forming or breaking habits because this will definitely speed up the process. But, however long it takes, if it moves you closer to your dreams it will be worth it.

Growing up in the 1980s, one of the earliest things I remember buying with my pocket money was a record. My sister and I were allowed to choose one 'single' (for younger readers, that was a vinyl record, seven inches in size, which had a song on either side and could be played, usually only in the living room, on a record player). The first record I remember buying was by Madonna. Madonna is an American singer and when I was a child, she was the artist whose records I wanted to buy!

At the time I write this, according to another of my trusty research assistants, Wikipedia, Madonna is the fourth best-selling music artist worldwide and is referred to as 'The Queen of Pop'. One thing that Madonna is renowned for, and to which she attributes much of her success, is reinventing herself. She has been selling 'records' for four decades. Not only has Madonna mastered the art of harnessing her inner confidence to achieve what she wants in life, she has kept on achieving, growing and evolving, continually trying new things which, it would be reasonable to assume, have taken her out of her comfort zone.

A more recent example of such an artist is Lady Gaga, who has also learnt the art of reinventing herself to stay in the spotlight and achieve longevity in an industry notorious for short-lived success. Her persona in *Poker Face,* which was released in 2008, is far removed from that of Shallow (*A Star Is Born*) ten years later.

This illustrates another interesting point: we are continually changing and evolving. Any labels that you have given yourself over the years that are holding you back can be peeled off and replaced with a new narrative that better fits the person you are, or the person you want to be, today.

One of the most marvellous facts of life is that you can, at any point, start something fresh. At the turn of a new calendar year, many of us think about forming new habits such as eating more healthily, going to the gym, taking up a new hobby or giving up smoking. But we don't need New

Year's Day to implement new habits that will make a positive impact on the way we live; we can do it at any time we choose, just like Madonna or Lady Gaga did.

It is on that note that we will conclude the second step in the process. Just do it, YabadabaDoit, authentically and with finesse.

When you are ready and you want to step out of the realms of comfort, remember all the tools you have in your toolbox:

- Breathe
- Smile
- Take up space, hold your head up high and stand tall
- Rationalise your thoughts, constructively challenge any negative self-talk and talk yourself up! Just be your own bestie
- Keep hydrated
- Invent and re-invent yourself; remember, you are exactly the person you choose to be!

Don't forget:

- Visualisation
- Purpose, drive, willpower and discipline aka – your inner army
- Your anchor

and Yabadabadoit! You will Yabadabadoit best when you remember why you are sending yourself out of your comfort zone in the first place.

As you did after the first step, why not take a few moments here to write down your thoughts. What do you intend to implement from this chapter? How will you go about it and when will you take action?

_____

_____

_____

_____

_____

_____

_____

_____

_____

_____

_____

_____

Review

'Change is the only constant in life'
Heraclitus

It is important to self-evaluate and be self-aware. Just as the world is constantly turning, you are constantly evolving, constantly learning and absorbing information, continually being exposed to new things and therefore in a constant state of change.

Testament to me being an advocate for getting out of my comfort zone is that I have worked in numerous different industry sectors over the years. That has given me the opportunity to see success, particularly in the business world, from different perspectives and viewpoints.

Perspective, and the ability to see things from another's viewpoint, is extremely valuable and, in my opinion, one of the crucial elements to emotional intelligence.

One job I had was working for an energy management software company for a short period around seven or eight years ago. Our motto as a business was 'You can't manage what you can't measure'. It helped us highlight the benefits of using software to measure, and therefore manage, energy consumption.

At that time energy largely came from finite resources and was steadily rising in cost. Our motto that we used so regularly gave our customers and prospective customers the reason why they needed to have access to our software in a single sentence. Interestingly, given my exposure to sayings and mottos from a young age, I hadn't come across this one in any other context before, but I have applied it many times since and it is relevant to managing your confidence.

The third step, review, brings us full circle in our quest to achieve. At the start of this book we explored why achieving beats winning every time on a personal level (there are no losers with achieving!). If you have absorbed everything in this book and put it into practice, formed several new habits whilst un-forming any unhelpful habits along the way, you will be well on your way to achieving.

However, we are all human. Life is busy; our priorities change and it would be overly optimistic to think that you can just implement all of the steps and away you go. It is important we review, which means analysing our growth or our progress.

Your analysis should result in at least one of these two outcomes:

1)   You can congratulate yourself on what is going well and improve on it/do more of it.
2)   You can be really honest about the areas that haven't gone as well as you would have liked and go back to basics on the habits for success in those particular areas.

When we talk about setting goals in the corporate world, we talk about SMART objectives. If you haven't come across these, they simply offer a framework for setting goals in such a way that you can assess their impact easily and without ambiguity. The goals should be specific, measurable, achievable, realistic (sometimes the R is used as 'relevant') and timebound/time-related.

The most successful companies, sports teams, movie franchises, etc. often have the common trait of being agile. To be agile, you need to be able to self-analyse and **dial up the positives** whilst addressing the development areas. You can only do this if you measure, honestly review your performance and give yourself constructive feedback.

One of the best things you can do to keep improving performance is to savour how it feels when things have worked and use that feeling to stay on track. We have all experienced proud moments when we passed a test, baked a cake to perfection, finished a physical challenge. It's important to conserve those feelings so they can motivate us to step out of our comfort zones again and know that the rewards at the other side will be worth it. This knowledge is very valuable and must be guarded and protected. Knowledge is data that can help us make sound judgement calls. Hold that thought, as we will come back to data very soon!

The company I work for now organises annual sporting challenges for charity. These are optional for staff to participate in. A year ago, I took part in a challenge called Tough Mudder with a group of colleagues; it was an eight-mile race with obstacles, some of which were extremely challenging, especially if you are of average fitness. You crawl through mud, under barbed wire, through very dark tunnels, over large and difficult to negotiate obstacles and are submerged in ice cold, dirty water more than once – with some electric shocks thrown in! As I left the start line, I remember feeling quite nervous. It was too late to do anything about it, but I was seriously considering my choice in signing up.

The weather was awful; it was cold and raining, which made it even tougher (and muddier!). Fairly near the start, around the third or fourth obstacle, I had to slide down a chute into a skip full of ice-cold dirty water, swim under it and pull myself out the other side. My body went into shock as I hit the water and I lost all my senses momentarily. I emerged soaking, heavy with the water, shivering and a little disorientated. My wonderful colleagues spurred me on and, despite my lips going blue, several hours later I finished the challenge.

There were quite a few low points (some very low points) over the four or so hours it took me to complete the course and I seriously considered dropping out. That would have been difficult, though, when people had donated to charity in my name!

I remember my elation when I saw the last obstacle (the electric shock one). The end was in sight and I knew the worst was behind me. Exhausted, still shivering, still with my blue lips, I staggered to the finish line. It is amazing how quickly the discomfort disappears when you reach a finish line. I received a headband and a T-shirt with *Finisher* written on it, and I felt absolutely awesome!

That headband is another of my anchors and it takes pride of place on my dressing table. If ever I doubt my ability to do something that requires physical strength, all I need to do is put on that headband!

What experiences do you have that you can draw on to experience a feeling of accomplishment that you have savoured?

A common experience for women who have just given birth is that all the pain and fatigue disappear the moment they cross that birthing finish line and get to hold their new addition to the world.

If you have ever studied for a qualification, you will have had that feeling of relief and accomplishment when the final piece of coursework is submitted, or the final examination completed, and you are free from the grind of constant learning and revision.

The more metaphorical finishing lines you cross in life, the stronger your confidence muscle will grow as you build up more evidence and data to support your knowledge that you are an achiever.

What props do you have, or could you obtain, to remind you of your success in the way my Tough Mudder headband does? Certificates, trophies, thank-you notes, acknowledgements all count as anchors.

Be data
(em)powered

In reviewing your progress in terms of harnessing your inner confidence, it's important to pledge to be completely honest with yourself. You will have some days that are better than others and that's perfectly fine. It's exactly how it should be.

It is said that in today's world the most valuable commodity is data. This is a somewhat controversial topic and I do not intend to get into a debate about whether the amount of data held about us by the tech giants is providing us with more than it takes from us. There are many other people better informed than I am on the subject. What I will say is that companies that collect and use data effectively (I am sure you know the ones I am referring to – if not, try asking Alexa) have evolved and grown smarter, stronger and more profitable often extremely quickly.

There is a lesson to be learnt from this: **one of the most valuable things you can do for yourself is to learn to interpret and work with your own internal data.** This includes your thoughts, feelings, responses, actions and reactions.

I truly believe that everything we go through – every experience, conversation, event, encounter, thought, no matter how fleeting, whether good, bad or ugly – gives us valuable data that we can use to continually develop.

You don't have to look back far in time to see that we humans are constantly evolving. Think back to those personal bests achieved in sports. It was 1954 when the record for the fastest mile on foot was broken; the four-minute 'barrier' was breached by a fraction of a second. That instilled faith that it could be done and it was not insurmountable. It took one man to break the record; now we have many women and men who can accomplish the once 'impossible' feat.

From a personal perspective, know that you are growing, always improving, and you have the power each day to be better, more prepared and faster than you were yesterday. Your capabilities are not finite, quite the opposite. No matter what stage of life you are at, you have no idea of your power and ability to do things until you try.

Even if you don't get the result you wanted when you try, I can promise that you will get data: data on how it felt; how you approached it; how you would do it differently next time, and how much it means to you to keep trying.

Those who improve over time are the ones who pay attention to their internal data, interpret it and work with it. There is a phrase that I have come to use as a mantra for my own personal development journey: **'I am smarter and stronger that I was yesterday, but tomorrow I will be stronger and smarter still'**.

I truly believe that this can be the case for every one of us. We control the intellectual property to our internal data;

through awareness of what it is telling us and by using it appropriately, we can make this statement true. If you choose to work with your own data and use it, your value will increase every day!

As we established earlier, mindfulness has become very popular in recent years as a tool to relieve stress and anxiety and improve wellbeing. Part of the practice of being mindful lies in noticing your thoughts. As a novice, you are taught just to notice without any response, judgement or reaction. If you can get used to doing that and notice the data you are being given so you can interpret it, you can use it to continually improve your confidence.

The techniques we have talked about centre around talking to yourself rationally whenever a lack of confidence or a 'bout of doubt' sets in. If you doubt yourself or lack belief in your abilities, notice it so that you can get to work on establishing why that feeling has come about. That will make it easier to determine which of the practices and techniques in this book are most appropriate to overcome a particular issue and restore confidence and faith in your abilities, getting you back on track to achieving all of your goals.

It is also worth asking yourself why doubt has set in at that particular time. Is there something going on, or something that has happened, that has impacted on your ability to focus on a positive outcome? The more you understand how and why you are reacting to situations that have put you under pressure to perform, the easier it becomes to bring out that inner army of Purpose, Drive, Willpower and

Discipline to overcome any doubts and step over them to accomplish what you want in life.

Keep it simple
and keep it up!

As I've already said, I like keeping things simple. Processes are handy for keeping things straightforward and simple. If there is a process to follow, people tend to get to the end result quickly without having to think too much. This is good because thinking too much at a time when you need to harness your inner confidence often manifests as procrastination. Procrastination is not something that will serve you well when you are trying to accomplish something.

I regard preparation as proactive, and proactivity as the antonym of procrastination. If you tend to procrastinate and you want to overcome it, your trusted friend proactivity can beat procrastination any day of the week – but only if you focus on it and you choose to empower it! You can only empower proactivity by taking action. It is a conscious choice, and it is your choice to make!

Proactivity can turn a 'bout of doubt' into a 'doubt drought'.

The process we can use to efficiently work through the three practices is to remember the elements of execution.

Elements of execution

Having practised these techniques for some time (maybe ten thousand hours over the years!), I can say from experience that the elements to keep in mind are Philosophy, Strategy and Action.

If we can nail the right philosophy we are empowered with knowledge, having thoughtfully asked the right questions and developed a sound strategy. Once you have a strategy, it's just a case of taking the appropriate action to get from where you are to where you want to be.

To bring this concept to life, let's use an example of buying a house. If you are renting your home and want to buy a house, you need to think about the best way to transition from tenant to homeowner.

Your philosophy will be to ask yourself the right questions and get clear answers. How much deposit will you need to save? How long will that take you? What is your ideal property? How much is it likely to cost? Where can you research how and where to find the ideal property? What insurances and other professional services might you need, and how will you determine which ones offer the best solution for your specific needs? What are the timescales you want to work to? What types of financing may be accessible to you and how will you determine which option suits you best? There will be many questions such as these that you will need to consider as you start the process.

Once you have clear answers to your questions, you can formulate your strategy. You need to save £x amount in order to have, for example, a 10% deposit for the type of house you want in the ideal location so you can commute to work and be close enough to the people and places you have identified as being important. You have set up a savings account for your deposit and cut back on your spending to ensure you can save enough by your target date. You have shortlisted estate agents, conveyancing professionals, insurance companies and mortgage lenders who could meet your needs, and worked out a plan to contact them for quotes. You have worked out how much notice you will need to give your landlord on your rented property, and set up alerts about homes that fall within your parameters when they come to the market. At this stage, you have a clear plan to get from tenant to homeowner. All of this means that you have a sound strategy.

The final part is the action. That requires you to keep saving in your savings account, and select and instruct the right third parties to help you at appropriate times to ensure that you are on track. Check out the new properties that might be your dream home so you can check that your plans and budget still align with your desired outcome and you will gain momentum towards the goal. Everything will fall into place from there.

Can you see how Philosophy and Strategy make the Action so much easier for the important things we want to achieve in life?

If we try and skip straight to Action, a hurdle we haven't thought about could show up at some stage – let's face it, that's life! The Philosophy and Strategy stages mean that if that happens, it is less likely to throw you off course because you have a plan in place.

In recent months I have been helping my teenage daughter with her schooling. Due to the UK being in lockdown because of the Covid-19 pandemic, she has suddenly found herself home-schooling. She asked me to read through a task for English, which was to complete some transactional writing. A question was posed about capital punishment and whether or not a country that used the death penalty could be considered civilised. She had to use a style of transactional writing to debate the point. Essentially, she had to pick one side and write either a speech, letter or article to validate her argument.

Keen to guide her to develop her own belief systems and have the confidence to argue for what she believes in, I asked her which side of the fence she was on. When she shared her thoughts, I helped her construct points to validate and support them.

The writer in me was keen to get straight to Action and help her articulate how she felt with passion and excitement. Knowing how such assignments work, she stopped me in my tracks. She showed me a page in her book with a list of transactional writing skills for each grade boundary. She started to ask questions about how she could achieve the marks required for her target grade, then spent a few minutes constructing a plan for the piece in order to attain a mark for each of the skills listed in her target grade boundary. She has been taught to think and do a little planning before jumping into the task; consequently, she had a sound Philosophy and Strategy before she leapt into Action.

She went on to produce a thought-provoking and heartfelt piece of writing that evidenced each skill required to get the highest grade. I was grateful for the reminder she gave me about the value of stepping back and taking preparation time. She really did remind me to practise what I preach, something that kids – especially teenagers in my experience – are superb at!

If we had done it my way, we would have still produced a thought-provoking and heartfelt piece but it may not have got her what she needed in terms of attainment. She may not have achieved what she wanted to from the task. By executing Philosophy and Strategy then jumping into Action, she got the optimum result.

Another good reason for using the three steps of execution is so that you don't find yourself in a situation where you are over-exerting your mental capacity because this could impact on your ability to perform and achieve what you want to achieve.

Something that has caught my attention over the past eighteen months or so, particularly as I have taken on more responsibility at work, is the concept of decision fatigue. I started to notice my own decision-making skills wavering later in the day and particularly at the end of a working week. I was curious why I was procrastinating more at certain times so I did a little research.

I have never been one who procrastinates so when I notice I am doing it through paying attention to my own internal data downloads, it's usually a signal that something is a little out of kilter.

Before reading up on it, I wouldn't have bought in to the concept of getting 'tired' from making decisions. However, having experienced it first hand when transitioning to a new role at work with more decision-making responsibilities than I was used to, I believe that it exists. I believe that the quality of your decision-making skills can be at risk of deteriorating if you have to make too many decisions in a short space of time. To effectively arrive at a sound decision, you have to weigh up everything, process possible outcomes, assess all possible impacts etc., which can be mentally taxing.

The purpose of sharing this with you is to illustrate the importance of prioritising where you direct your energy. Decision making is part of preparation and planning, and the quality of your decisions will impact the quality of your outcomes. For the big things you want to achieve, carve out enough space and time in your life to give them the best of yourself.

Going back to some of the earlier examples we talked through, such as going for a job interview or giving a presentation, there are a couple of hacks that can help you avoid decision fatigue on days when it's the last thing you will want. You can plan to keep decision making on the day of a key event to a minimum; for example, plan what you will wear the night before so you don't have to decide on the day; plan an alternate route should your train be delayed so it's not something you have to decide on the day. These are all things that are easier to do when you aren't under pressure to harness your confidence and get out of your comfort zone.

Your number one fan

Although we have three simple steps, we have touched on many different strategies to improve confidence levels, some of which you may wish to revisit either at crucial moments or as refreshers when you need them.

To consolidate our journey, I want to go back to perhaps the most important advice that we covered in this book. It underscores everything but most notably in the *Faith, establish your anchor* and *Be your own bestie* sections of the book.

The thing I want you to remember is this: when you accomplish something – and you will accomplish things each and every day, no matter how small – **savour the feeling and bank it.**

It is a source of sadness to me that some people brush aside the positives and focus on the negatives. I have seen this time and again in both professional and personal settings. So many people I have met downplay their achievements and talents, not stopping to congratulate themselves sufficiently on a job well done, not acknowledging their kind acts or the impact they have on those around them. This is not conducive to building inner confidence.

There is a saying you may have come across 'Energy flows where attention goes'. Where confidence is concerned, we can use this saying to its advantage. Your mind is super powerful; if you focus positively on your accomplishments, safe in the knowledge of what you can achieve, more accomplishments will follow.

Patting yourself on the back for a job well done is not big headed or egotistical; it is an effective tool to establish faith that you are capable, which you are! The best gift you can give to yourself is to allow yourself to feel proud when you achieve something that has taken you out of your comfort zone.

I also recommend that you look out for others in the same way. If you notice that someone has achieved something, tell them 'well done'. Call them what you want – high fives, champagne moments, pats on the back – these are what keep our desire to keep growing and achieving burning brightly.

Now is your time

Remember how I told you about the elderly people I cared for in one of the first jobs I did? Let's once again contemplate their responses to my question, 'Do you have any regrets?' They were along the lines of 'I wish I had followed my dreams more, not caring what others think'.

Implementing what we have explored on this journey will help you follow your own dreams, and those dreams are waiting for you **right now**. The reason I want you to pause and think about this is because so many people I have met have a propensity to wait, to put things off, to say they will do it 'one day' or 'some day'. How many times have you heard someone say, 'One day I will…?'

Whilst it's important to have things to look forward to in the future – and some things do take time to work towards – putting off your dreams and ambitions shouldn't be shelved for a later date. You have one precious lifetime. From the moment we are born, the clock ticks.

There will never be a 'right time' or a 'better time' to level up your confidence and go after what you want in life.

Now is the time.

Never stop achieving

'Success is a journey, not a destination.
Or maybe it's a 'learny' and you will be
forever the student'

As a child I was fairly good at running. I progressed from winning sports' day races in my infant years to representing my secondary school both as a sprinter and distance runner. I liked running, and I liked the satisfaction of reaching the finish line.

When I was about fourteen, I lost interest in the training sessions and spent the next twenty or so years not running much. Other hobbies, pastimes and life in general took my time and my attention.

Then my son started doing a couch to five kilometres to increase his stamina and fitness after resting because of shin splints. That reminded me that I used to like running and I used to be fairly good at it, so I asked him if I could tag along. And so tag along I did.

For the first couple of weeks I plodded along for a couple of kilometres before walking the rest of the way and meeting him back at home. If you haven't come across couch to five kilometres, I should explain that it's a running plan aimed at absolute beginners and any fitness level. It involves regular runs over a nine-week period, gradually building up from a little running with lots of walking to just running. As I understand it, couch to five kilometres was designed by a runner who wanted to help his mum get off the couch and start exercising. He designed the programme so she could follow it, and it has helped countless others ditch sedentary for stamina.

One of the things I value more than anything is the bond I have with my kids, so having a pastime with my adult son kept me motivated during those first couple of weeks. When I was questioning if I still liked running (and I was definitely questioning if I was still good at it) I had a pretty strong 'why'. This was a way to spend time with someone who means the world to me and have a common goal, something to chat about together.

Before long my fitness increased so that I could keep up (no more plodding) and enjoy running distances from five to ten kilometres regularly and with relative ease. As a surprising consequence, I also had the chance to bond with my daughter. Whilst I was re-igniting a childhood passion, I was also helping her with her revision for her science and physical education exams. We have been able to chat about how my resting heart rate has decreased significantly since I started running regularly and she can very accurately describe the reasons for that, as well as the benefits, that relate to her studies.

We all know that physical performance can be increased through training and commitment. Experience has taught me that mental performance can be enhanced in the same way. I recently heard that people are setting up 'mind-gyms', and I agree wholeheartedly that we need to keep healthy physically and mentally through exercising both our bodies and our minds. Whilst 'mind-gyms' might be a relatively new business idea, in reality we have been working out our mental muscles for a long time now with crosswords, puzzles, jigsaws, books and other such things that keep the mind sharp. So, from now on, I want you to think of your confidence like a muscle that needs to be trained, nurtured and looked after in order to keep performing at its optimal level.

On the back of my re-ignited pleasure in running, I have joined a social media group for female runners and am often inspired by the posts in the group. For example, a lady uploaded a screenshot of her route and time and a huge smiling selfie with the caption: *First ever 10k accomplished and I am 55 years old.*

I am not sure if people are getting braver and more determined to take all life has to offer or whether I'm just noticing it more as I get older, but I seem to hear and see more examples of great accomplishments by older people than ever before. I believe people everywhere are harnessing their inner-confidence to make the most of life by challenging stereotypes. It excites me to know that I live in a time where we are pushing boundaries, challenging the status quo and rebelling against expectations. How much can the collective consciousness of man (and woman and child, of course) achieve if we all get on board with that?

I sincerely hope that you now feel at least a tad braver, a bit more capable and a whole lot more inspired to go and grab everything you want. We have talked a lot about habits being the key to change, forming new positive new habits, breaking unhelpful habits, and so on. A great hack for implementing something once you feel inspired is to set yourself a timebound challenge.

As I mentioned to you, I have read a great many books. Some have fired me up to make a change in my life, only for me to forget much of the content as soon as they are back on the bookshelf.

Well done for investing the time in yourself to absorb the three-step process that will support your confidence breakthrough. Having reached the closing pages of this book, please take a moment to contemplate what you will carry forward into your everyday life.

To help you with this, I want to encourage you to set yourself a challenge that works for you, a bit like a couch to five kilometres. The challenge is best set *by* you and *for* you. Depending on where you are in your confidence journey, your life and what you want to achieve, you may need a seven-day challenge, a thirty-day challenge or perhaps longer.

I will share with you the fundamentals and you can create the detail that suits you best.

1) Make a note of what you want to achieve.
2) Set a reasonable timeframe to do it in.
3) Work out what steps you need to take to get from where you are now to achieving your goal.
4) At the start of each day, remind yourself of the goal and take whatever action you can to move towards it.
5) At the end of each day, congratulate yourself for any action you took that will help you move towards

what you have set out to achieve. If you haven't taken action that day, pledge to do so tomorrow!

6) Keep pushing forward. Remember that your goals may change and your course may meander, but that's okay!

You can create your own challenge and outline the specifics of how you will YabadabaDoIt below.

_____

_____

_____

_____

_____

_____

_____

_____

_____

_____

If you need further inspiration you can visit www.attitudeacademy.co.uk for support and insights.

I want to conclude now by thanking you for being a part of my Yabadabadoit journey and share a few words to leave you pondering.

Confidence is something that, if nurtured, will grow and get stronger and shine brighter. Feed it, and water it, love it, believe in it, protect it and guide it, give it plenty of exposure to the light, rest it when you need to and be grateful for the power you have within that it affords to you, for you were born with everything you will ever need to realise your dreams; they won't fall in your lap though as there would be no fun in that, you have to go out there, in to the vast unknown, and make your best life happen.

Printed in Great Britain
by Amazon

87537158R00068